A Mouse in th

Hidden M

By

Jeremy J. Warner

ISBN 978-0-9853555-0-0

Published by Portrait Health Publishing, Inc.
2201 Waukegan Road, Suite 170
Bannockburn, IL 60015
www.portraithealthpublishing.com

Cover Design and Interior Graphics by Danielle Warner

Disclaimer

This book makes references to various Disney copyrighted characters, trademarks, marks, and registered marks owned by the Walt Disney Company and Disney Enterprises, Inc. All references to these properties are made solely for editorial purposes. Neither the author nor the publisher makes any commercial claim to their use, and neither is affiliated with the Walt Disney Company in any way.

Table of Contents

Chapter 1. A Mouse's Tale

These are the adventures of a small mouse named Joey. Now Joey was no ordinary mouse. He was one of the biggest Disney fans in the mouse world. He holds the mouse record of riding Space Mountain thirty seven times in one day. Even though Joey was only four years old, which is around eighteen in human years, he devoted his entire life to finding Hidden Mickeys throughout the Disney parks. What is a Hidden Mickey you ask?

A Hidden Mickey is an image of Mickey Mouse concealed in the design of a Disney attraction or resort. Traditionally, it takes the shape of Mickey's head and ears in silhouette, one large circle with two smaller circles on top, but Hidden Mickeys can also take on many forms to resemble the most famous mouse in the world.

Joey idolized Mickey Mouse. In fact, he would do anything possible to trade lives with Mickey. He even spends two hours per day working on imitating Mickey's voice. "Ha ha... oh, boy!" Joey exclaimed trying to show off his best Mickey voice. However, it sounded like nothing more than a mousy falsetto.

Today was a special day because Joey had a blind date with a mouse he had met on Rodent Relations, a popular online dating service in the mouse world. Knowing that she was a huge Disney fan, he couldn't think of a better gift than putting together a complete list of all of the Hidden Mickeys throughout the Magic Kingdom and presenting it to her. After all, he believed that Hidden Mickeys were a tribute to mice all over the world. And, Joey had not been on a date since his bad break up with one of the hula girls from "it's a small world". But more on that after a monorail ride around the Seven Seas Lagoon, which is where our story begins.

Chapter 2. Main Street U.S.A

Joey awoke from a deep sleep to the sound of the monorail conductor, "please stand clear of the doors. Por favor, mantengase alejado de las puertas." In an effort to be one of the first guests at the Magic Kingdom, Joey decided the night before to sleep on the purple monorail in a hole in one of the seats. His hair was messy and he had dark circles under his eyes, but it was worth it to start off his hunt for Hidden Mickeys throughout the park.

Walt Disney World Railroad

Joey wanted to plan out his route perfectly to make sure he could hit every ride in the Magic Kingdom. After all, there are so many tributes to mice throughout the park, he felt it would be wrong not to see every one. So, he decided to ride the Walt Disney World Railroad and take in the beauty of the park.

Before heading up the stairs to the loading platform of the train station, Joey looked up at the roof of the Main Street Station and found a Hidden Mickey designed in scrollwork. The entire roof was covered in scrollwork and each individual segment formed a Hidden Mickey.

Satisfied with his discovery, Joey boarded the antique steam-powered train and sat back to enjoy the ride.

Main Street, U.S.A
After a full lap of the park on the railroad, Joey headed down Main Street, U.S.A to find some more Hidden treasures. While looking down at the ground right at the entrance of the park, he noticed the reflection from the street lamps all form Hidden Mickeys.

Main Street Vehicles

The sounds of bells and hooves grabbed Joey's attention as he continued down Main Street, U.S.A. As the large stallions passed by, he found a couple Hidden Mickeys on the bridle gear on the horses pulling the trolley car.

He wrote down his discoveries in the journal he was creating for his blind date and continued on.

Tony's Town Square Restaurant

The smell of horses quickly changed to an Italian pasta sauce coming from Tony's Square Restaurant. "This restaurant looks like it was the place where Lady and the Tramp shared spaghetti and their first kiss!" Joey's mouth started to water as he ran in to find three white flowers perfectly situated to form a Hidden Mickey to the upper left of the bookshelf as he entered the main dining area.

As he walked over to get a closer look, there was a tiny impression on a black tile below his feet that formed a classic Mickey. The tile was located to the left as he entered the seating area. It was the second black tile from the rear wall, against the left wall.

Impressed with how much progress he had made finding Hidden Mickeys, Joey decided to stay for a bowl of pasta... extra cheese.

Chapter 3.   Tomorrowland

It was nearly eleven o'clock in the morning when Joey finished up his mid-morning breakfast at Tony's. Not wanting to waste any more time, he headed over to Tomorrowland to continue the search for Hidden Mickeys.

Carousel of Progress

Joey loved the fact that shining at the end of every day is a great big beautiful tomorrow. So he went to the Carousel of Progress, chose his seat as the audience chairs began to rotate around the stage as the show began. A couple minutes into the show, there was a scene where the daughter was getting ready to go out for Valentine's Day. A Mickey made of cloth right at the top of the mirror became visible as the lights turned on.

In the middle of the show, the second scene, Joey found another Hidden Mickey hiding in the background. It was a bronze, pitcher-shaped wall hanging in the sink area which looked like the profile of Mickey.

As the show continued, Joey laughed as the girl tried to lose weight on the shaker machine. It was then he noticed Mickey's sorcerer's hat on the right side of the room.

The seats turned again to the dining room scene, and on the right rear wall was a picture of Mickey from the Sorcerer's Apprentice. On the left side of the room, a Mickey nutcracker was situated on left of the mantel. And under the Christmas tree there was a box with a plush Mickey Mouse.

Towards the end of the show, a classic Mickey appeared on the top of a spaceship in the middle of the television screen. When Grandma started playing the video game, Joey found it on the television screen for a very brief moment.

Tomorrowland Speedway

Having trouble getting the Carousel of Progress song out of his head, Joey decided he felt like taking a drive. Since there is no age limit on the Tomorrowland Speedway, he raced over to get in line and noticed on the ground a shadow that resembled Mickey himself. When he looked up, Joey found that the three circular globes that house the lights high on the light poles casted a shadow to create this magic.

And then as he looked over to the tables right outside the ride, he could see that the table umbrellas were positioned perfectly so they formed multiple Hidden Mickeys.

Joey finally got in his mini race car after a 15 minute wait. "I don't want to brag, but I am a pretty good driver for a mouse," Joey exclaimed as he revved his engine. His car took off in a shot and as he came around one of the turns, there were several billboard type segments on the back wall. The middle billboard showed a smoke trail of a very fast car. There appeared to be a few small black outlines of cheering fans. The second fan to the right was wearing a small pair of Mickey ears!

Astro Orbiter

Now that Joey drove the Tomorrowland Speedway at the age of four, he felt like he needed to accomplish something bigger. Something better! So he decided to be the first mouse in space. He headed over to the Astro Orbiters and found a small classic Mickey in the cement close to a support beam.

As Joey got in line and waited for the elevator to take him to his rocket ship, he saw the planets spinning above. Just then, the planets aligned to form one large circle, with 2 small ones at the proper angle to resemble a Hidden Mickey.

Cosmic Ray's Starlight Café

Traveling through space can make a small mouse hungry, so Joey went over to his friend Cosmic Ray's Starlight Café for some cheesy bread. He grabbed a table close to the stage, frightened some over-sensitive tourists while they were eating, and began to watch the show. It was then he noticed that on the star dome on the right, center edge, three stars made up a Hidden Mickey.

Buzz Lightyear's Space Ranger Spin

After dinner and show at Comic Ray's, Joey was ready to return to space and help Buzz Lightyear fight the forces of evil. As he entered the line to blast off, Joey enjoyed the posters on the wall and found that in the second poster, Sector 1 is a Mickey profile and Sector 2, the planets form a classic Mickey.

Another poster showed the Planets of the Galactic Alliance. There was a green planet that showed the shape of Mickey himself.

Joey boarded his space cruiser at Start Command and blasted off into space. While traveling through the galaxy, Joey entered a

Battery Room and found Mickey's profile under "Initiate Battery Unload".

Then he came to a room with fireworks on the wall. Some of the fireworks aligned to form a Hidden Mickey.

As his space cruiser returned to earth, Joey was granted the title of Junior Space Ranger. "What a great ride!" Joey said feeling the effects of the happiest place on earth.

Joey wanted to remember his journeys through space, so he went over to the Ride Photo Area to pick up his space photo and found a yellow Mickey across from the monitors. He also found where they had locked Zurg behind bars, and found the star field on right was another classic Mickey.

Monsters, Inc. Laugh Floor

Now Joey loved to laugh. So after an adventuresome journey through space, he got in line at the Monsters, Inc. Laugh Floor. There on the wall was a Recreational Rocket picture where the moon craters were shaped like upside-down Mickeys. Also on the walls was a Space Collectibles Convention Sign. In this image, the asteroids were shaped like a classic Mickey.

The comedy club was hopping as Mike Wazowski brought down the house.

Space Mountain

Feeling the need for speed, Joey wanted to take another journey through space at Space Mountain. As he waited in line to board the rocket ship, a news report came on the screen. In the report, a satellite came towards the camera that he was sure was in the shape of Mickey's head.

He also noticed that every third window of stars while he waited in line was a Mickey constellation.

On the ride, while trying to hold on, Joey opened his eyes for a brief moment and found that the speakers on the ride vehicles were in the shape of a Mickey.

Tomorrowland Transit Authority PeopleMover

After zipping through space, Joey needed some time to catch his breath. So he boarded the blue train... at least, that's what he liked to call it. When going through one of the tunnels, he found a classic Mickey on the belt buckle of the woman getting her hair done.

Then as the mass transit system turned a corner and passed by the Tomorrowland stage, he found a large Mickey above the stage. It was made out of the scaffolding.

Joey then found another great view of the firework Mickeys on the Buzz Lightyear ride while going through one of the tunnels.

The blue train returned to the station and Joey exited the ride.

Mickey's Star Traders Shop

Joey's philosophy is that you can't go to the most magical place on earth without bringing home a few souvenirs. So he headed over to Mickey's Star Traders and instantly noticed the satellite dishes on the wall formed a Mickey icon.

In another part of the store, there was a mural on the wall where Mickey hats sit atop windows halfway up the sides of the building. The top of the building in the mural resembled a Mickey.

Chapter 4. Liberty Square

When Joey was only one year old, he went on the Haunted Mansion ride, and it was so scary, he has not been back since. "We have had nine hundred and ninety nine happy haunts, but there's room for a thousand. Any volunteers?" The spooky voice from the Haunted Mansion continued to play over and over in Joey's head. But, he was on a mission of love and exploration and couldn't afford to skip one of the best rides in the park.

The Haunted Mansion

Trying to gather his nerves, Joey made the decision to ride the Haunted Mansion. As he entered the mansion he gazed at the aging man over the fireplace. His fears went instantly out of mind when the found that the boarder of the picture was designed with numerous Hidden Mickeys.

Starting to build up his confidence, he moved over to the other side of the foyer, and found a candle lamp on the wall that seemed perfectly normal. But upon further inspection, Joey realized that if you stand with your back to the wall and look up at the base of the lamp, the candle holders on the lamp form Hidden Mickeys.

Joey found himself in a room with no windows, and no doors. In an ominous voice a Ghost Host offered him a chilling challenge, "to find a way out!" The Ghost Host offered "his way", but that was something Joey was afraid to discuss in detail. So instead, he escaped the morbid room and boarded a doom buggy. As he rode past an endless hallway, he found that the back of the purple chair formed an abstract Donald Duck. Near the top of the chair, he could see Donald's cap, which sat above his distorted eyes, face and bill. Though it was not a mouse, Joey was happy with this discovery as his third cousin once removed was a duck.

The doom buggy turned a hall past a group of doors where the door knockers were knocking and pulsing. At the end of the hall was a sign that read "Tomb Sweet Tomb." There Joey found several bunches of flowers around the border of the sign. The bottom, center bunch created a Hidden Mickey.

Joey then found himself in the banquet hall. As the ghosts began to come alive in the room, he found that one of the plate settings on the table formed a Hidden Mickey.

As if the main part of the house was not scary enough, Joey ventured up to the attic with a corpse bride and discovered three pots formed a classic Hidden Mickey on the vertical beam.

The ghosts became too much for Joey, so he escaped through a window into the grave yard. When he came upon a female opera singer, the Grim Reaper to next to her was holding a Hidden Mickey in his left hand. Joey had to look back to see it clearly in the tomb.

Before exiting the ride, Joey was warned by the Ghost Host to beware of hitchhiking ghosts. As you can imagine, this made him pee a little, so he ran out of the doom buggy and while exiting, noticed that the last hanging light fixture before going outside formed a Hidden Mickey shadow on the ceiling. He continued to run as fast as possible to get away from the hitchhiking ghosts and found a classic Mickey lock holding the gate open.

Finally outside and away from the mansion, Joey breathed a sigh of relief.

Liberty Tree Tavern Restaurant

Just outside the mansion, the smell of spices coming from the Liberty Tree Tavern Restaurant was almost overwhelming. Joey entered the tavern and found in the waiting area a spice rack on the back wall right hand side which had three grapes painted into a Mickey.

Impressed with this discovery, he took a picture and stayed for a refreshment.

Liberty Square Riverboat

Feeling the need to get out on the open water, Joey went over to the Liberty Square Riverboat and entered the line. There he found the locks on the stocks near the entrance formed a Hidden Mickey.

After boarding the paddlewheel steamship, he sat back and enjoyed the sounds and smell of fresh air.

The Hall of Presidents

Now there are millions of mice throughout the United States, but no mouse is more patriotic than Joey. So, he raced over to the Hall of Presidents to scope out the Hidden Mickeys. Sure enough, in the waiting area there was a painting of George Washington.

Looking very closely at the tip of his sword Joey realized it formed a classic Hidden Mickey.

Soon the crowd began to enter the theater and President Obama appeared on the stage. The lace on the table cloth next to President Obama formed classic Hidden Mickeys.

As to be expected, Joey fell asleep half way through the speeches.

Columbia Harbor House Restaurant

As the show came to an end, the growling of Joey's stomach startled him awake. So, he headed over to the Columbia Harbor House Restaurant and went to the downstairs dining area. On the wall he found a map when viewed from the cash registers appeared to be Mickey's head.

Enjoying the savory smell of the food, Joey went up to the second floor of the Harbor House and discovered three large marble-like balls in a fishing net arranged to form a Mickey head. The blue marble was Mickey's head and the two black ones were his ears.

Chapter 5. Frontierland

Every time Joey visited the Magic Kingdom on vacation, he was too scared to ride Thunder Mountain. After all, it was the wildest ride in the wilderness. Something about the speed of the train made his little mouse knees shake. But, today he was ready to take the plunge and give it a try.

Big Thunder Mountain Railroad

The best seat on Thunder Mountain is the last mine car. So Joey waited in line and requested the back row from the cast member helping the guests board the ride.

The train started to climb the first hill as Joey held on to his hat and glasses. He felt a rush of excitement and nervous anticipation as the front of the train started to slowly begin the drop. The out of control mine car raced all over the mountain and before he knew it, he was at the end of the ride passing a bunch of dinosaur bones when on the ground he found three rusty gears, one much larger than the other two which formed a perfect Hidden Mickey.

Proud of himself for braving one of the fastest rides in the park, Joey headed out the exit with a big mouse smile on his face and found three cacti just outside the exit in the shape of a Hidden Mickey.

Could the day get any better?

Tom Sawyer Island

Joey had always heard a rumor that there was another Hidden Mickey on the side of Big Thunder Mountain, which could only be seen from Tom Sawyer Island. So he took a raft across the Rivers of America to an island and found himself at the side of the fort that was closest to Thunder Mountain. Looking out the hole of the gun turret on the right, he looked for a small white area on the mountain. There he saw three rocks in the shape of a Mickey head, almost sideways! It appeared to be the only white spot in that area.

Feeling like Huckleberry Finn, Joey entered the middle Rifle Roost at the entrance to Fort Langhorn. On a handrail towards the top of the tower, there was a Hidden Mickey created by a wood knot, an additional mark and an impression in the wood. Joey grabbed his camera, and snapped off a picture of this Hidden treasure.

Rivers of America

Since mice are terrible swimmers, Joey was excited to return to dry land. He exited the raft after returning from Tom Sawyer's Island, and proceeded along the dock. Looking back at the small shack on the neighboring dock, he saw a fishing net containing three glass globe fishing floats arranged as Mickey.

He then continued down the ramp to the dock where he found the break room door with three pulleys. They appeared to form the shape of the three circles for Mickey's head.

Country Bear Jamboree

It was now late in the afternoon, and Joey was starting to get tired. So he stopped at the closest turkey leg vendor, grabbed an oversized piece of bird and decided he would take in a show. Nothing compared to a jolly band of bears singing a Jamboree. So Joey took his seat at the Country Bear Jamboree in Grizzly Hall Theater and while looking at the stage, noticed that at the top center of the stage, there was a Hidden Mickey formed by a flower and scroll.

And now on with the show!

Splash Mountain

Ready to tackle another one of his fears, Joey ran over to Splash Mountain because he was told there are tons of Hidden Mickeys to be found. He entered the line and immediately saw a red Hidden Mickey painted on a yoke hanging on the left wall of the first tunnel in the queue.

While still in line, he passed an acorn house in one of the trees. Looking at the side of the house, just below the roof he found a large acorn with two smaller ones that formed a classic Mickey.

Finally he made it to the front of the line and prepared to board one of the hollowed-out logs. Before getting on the ride, Joey turned and looked at the wall behind him and saw several large holes that looked like a boulder crashed into it. Three holes seemed to come together to make the impression of a giant Hidden Mickey.

Joey was excited (and scared) because he got the front row. As the log climbed the mountain and made it to the first outside part of ride, he looked to his right before making the right u-shaped turn and passed by an upright barrel with "Muskrat Moonshine" painted on the side. Right on the front of the barrel was a perfect Hidden Mickey located above the "s" in Muskrat.

Joey's tiny mouse stomach tightened as he braved the first big drop. "Not sure why they call this the laughing place, that drop almost made me cry!" Joey said. While passing Brer Frog, he found that the bobbers in the water were in the shape of a Hidden Mickey.

Now was time for the true test. The largest drop in the park. The log began to climb up the never ending mountain. Joey couldn't determine what was scarier…. the size of the drop, or the vultures that looked like they wanted to eat him. But to his surprise, he noticed the hole in the rock formed the side profile of Mickey right before you plummet to your death. Joey also noticed this when standing outside the ride watching others take the plunge.

The log dove down the enormous drop and came shooting out the other side of the briar patch. "This water tastes terrible," Joey said realizing he forgot to keep him mouth closed at the end of the drop.

Not sure if he survived or went to heaven, Joey found himself in the middle of clouds and a musical dance number when he saw in the clouds Mickey lying on his back.

To his relief, the ride was over and he had survived another big ride at the park.

Walt Disney Railroad and Depot

Ready for another train ride, Joey went over to the entrance to the Frontierland train station. He found cactus plants growing in a unique formation. The one on the far right appeared to be in the shape of two ears and a head.

Happy with his continued success finding Hidden mice, he rode the train around the entire park taking in the scenery.

Frontierland Shootin' Arcade

Even a mouse needs to get out a little heat rage from the Florida sun. Joey couldn't think of anything better than firing some guns over at the Frontierland Shootin' Arcade. As he picked up his rifle, he aimed at the far left of the target area for a group of small cacti. One cactus near the middle of this group was shaped like a Hidden Mickey.

Chapter 6. Fantasyland

Even a mouse wants to feel like a Prince who lives in a large castle. Where better to imagine your life as a Prince or Princess than in a fairy-tale fortress guarding the entrance to Fantasyland?

Cinderella's Castle

Joey moved up the walkway to Cinderella's Castle and along the way saw three-circle patterns in the stone railings along the walkway. The sun was hitting them just right this early afternoon to see Mickey formed by shadows on the ground. Not everyone can find this one, but Joey knew if you timed it just right, you could see the magic.

Taking in the immense size of this medieval fortress, Joey looked up at the balconies on the side of the castle. The front part of each balcony seemed to have upside-down Mickey heads cut out of the stone.

Joey walked through Cinderella's Castle until he reached the Villain's store. Outside the store was a mailbox with a Hidden Mickey towards the bottom.

"This really is a fairy tale come true!" Joey said with joy.

Prince Charming Regal Carrousel

Joey was a huge fan of horses and spinning, so he ran over to the Prince Charming Regal Carrousel. As he rode the largest horse he could find up and down, he gazed at the mirrors surrounding the center part of the Carrousel. The etchings at the top of the mirrors made perfect Mickeys.

The antique carrousel came to stop, and Joey headed on to the next ride.

"it's a small world"

Joey could recite all of words to "it's a small world" by heart. This was because he made the Hawaii section his home for many months when he accidentally fell in love with one of the Hula girls.

Looking up at the entrance sign with a reminiscent look on his face, he found that the scrollwork sign supports were Mickey's ears forming a classic Mickey.

Joey was fortunate enough to get the front row of the boat. As he sailed into the Africa Room he looked at the vines above the giraffe which had purple leaves shaped like Mickey heads.

Then, in the South Pacific Room he found that the Koala bears on the left had Hidden Mickeys on the back of their heads.

Joey hid his face as he passed the Hula Girl from his past. Let's just say, his relationship did not end so well, but that is a different story. "Who breaks up with someone via text message... from their girlfriend's mom?" Joey mumbled under his breath as he passed her.

Seeing the irony of learning dozens of ways to say goodbye at the end of the ride, he got out of the boat and headed up the exit ramp. On the wall were paintings of Nutcrackers. While looking closely, he saw that their eyes and noses made the common Hidden Mickey and the helmets they were wearing made the smiley mouth.

Fairytale Garden

Realizing he hadn't collected any character autographs, Joey got in line at Fairytale Garden to see who he could meet. At the base of the first light pole on the right as he entered, a classic Mickey was hiding in the cement.

He grabbed an autograph from Snow White and continued on his hunt.

Mickey's PhilharMagic

Joey always heard that Mickey's PhilharMagic was an incredible 3D show at the Magic Kingdom. Not wasting any time, he ran in line and found a mural with a white classic Mickey.

When he grabbed his seat, in the front row of course, he put on his 3D opera glasses and found the right screen border had a classic Mickey hiding inside a French horn.

Peter Pan's Flight

Mickey's PhilharMagic created many happy thoughts, so it only made sense for Joey to make his way over to Peter Pan's Flight. While in the entrance queue he noticed that the fourth tree from the far end had a classic Mickey.

Even the clouds on the entrance sign formed a classic Mickey. Though the sign had changed since the last time he was there, he still found a side Mickey Hidden in a cloud under a lamp. The face and nose were recessed and the ears were sticking out.

Joey boarded a pirate galleon and began flying over London. As he passed the mermaids, he looked down to find a Hidden Mickey painted on the mountain as one of the flowers. He had to look back a little to see it, but it was definitely there.

While flying over the Jolly Roger where the pirates were defeated by Peter Pan, there was a stack of cannon balls on the deck. The shadow formed a perfect Mickey icon.

As the pixie dust wore off, Joey's flight came to an end and he exited the ride.

Snow White's Scary Adventures

There was a rumor going around that one of Joey's favorite rides, Snow White, was going to be torn down. So Joey grabbed his camera and went to say his goodbyes.

Looking at the mural in the waiting area, he found shorts on the clothes line with tiny, red Mickey heads. Also on the mural he noticed the chimney stones formed Mickeys.

Boarding the mine car, he entered the castle where the Wicked Queen was looking in the mirror. At the top of the mirror, 3 circles formed a classic Mickey.

In one of the next rooms, Joey saw a green turtle trying to climb a flight of stairs. On the turtle's back, the circles clearly formed a Hidden Mickey.

As the ride ended, a tear streamed down Joey's face as he realized this would be the last time he would get to journey on this classic ride.

Mad Tea Party

Since Joey was already crying, he thought it would be a great opportunity to make himself throw up on the Tea Cups. As he spun his worries away, he noticed a Hidden Mickey was formed by the three spinning disks that moved the cups around.

"This feels like a very unbirthday!"

Now that Joey had lost most of his lunch, he thought, "why not get a table at the most expensive restaurant in the park, Cinderella's Royal Table?"

Cinderella's Royal Table

There were no more reservation times available at Cinderella's Royal Table, so Joey jumped up on one of the tables scaring away most of the guests. This was not very nice, but he was quite hungry from losing his lunch on the Tea Cups. He started on a half-eaten steak when a female cast member came by with an inverted Mickey made of roses on the outside cuff of her costume sleeve. "Would you like something from the dessert tray?" she asked.

Joey made a note of this new Hidden Mickey and headed out of the restaurant.

The Many Adventures of Winnie the Pooh

Joey was full from an excellent meal and came up with a great idea. "Let's go bouncing with Tigger!" He boarded Pooh's hunny pot and found himself in Rabbit's garden where a small marker with radishes had one radish shaped like a Mickey.

He then came to the scene with Pooh in the Honey Tree. Looking very closely at Pooh on the left side of his head, there was a Hidden Mickey in the honeycomb.

Towards the end of the ride, Joey noticed a honey pot that had over flowed. Some of the dripping formed a Mickey head.

Joey took a picture of the Hidden Mickey and made his way over to Adventureland.

Chapter 7. Adventureland

According to pirate legend, dead men tell know tales. But they do hide a lot of Hidden Mickeys! And Joey was not ashamed to admit that he was a huge Caption Jack Sparrow fan. He had the hat, the outfit, and his impersonation was uncanny. Singing the Yo Ho Yo Ho a Pirate's Life For Me theme song, he got in line for one of the best rides in the Magic Kingdom.

Pirates of the Caribbean

As Joey twisted and turned throughout the entrance line, he stopped at a tall gun cabinet locked with Mickey locks.

He made a couple more turns in line where he ended up at cannon balls configured as a classic Mickey.

Joey's good fortune continued as he once again got the front row. As the boat sailed through wretched pirates, he came upon a drunken pirate with a cat sitting over his shoulder. As he looked at the wall, he noticed the cat casted a classic Mickey shadow on the wall.

As the ride came to an end, some pirates were locked up in a jail cell. Keeping the door secure was a Mickey-shaped lock.

In the very next room, Captain Jack Sparrow was sitting in a chair surrounded by gold and jewels. The top of the back of his chair had a classic Hidden Mickey in plain sight.

"...but you have heard of me," Joey said in his best Jack Sparrow voice.

Jungle Cruise

Joey wanted a ride with less rough waters ahead. He also loved animals so he thought, "What better way to see jungle animals without the risk of being eaten than to ride the Jungle Cruise?" The line was quite long, so Joey had time to stare at the entrance sign and found another Hidden Mickey under the "J" in Jungle Cruise.

The line seemed to speed along and before he knew it, Joey was sailing on a tramp-steamer down the rivers of Africa and passing a group of rhinos. On the ground he found three black rocks which formed a classic Mickey.

The boat continued to speed past a waterfall and on the left hand side there was a plane. Looking to the lower right of the plane, Joey found white circles that made up a Hidden Mickey.

As the boat sailed through an ancient temple, Joey noticed that the undecorated column they passed had a chipped area of brick on the third block from the top forming a Hidden Mickey.

The skipper guided the guests safely back to shore, and Joey headed out for his next adventure.

Swiss Family Treehouse

Feeling the urge to climb, Joey raced over to the Swiss Family Treehouse and began a trek up the side of the tree. He walked around the trunk of the tree before getting to the first official room. On the side of the tree was a side silhouette of Mickey. It was white with green moss splotched on it. He also noticed another way to find it was by looking up at the prayer room and finding an oar sticking out of the bottom. The blade of the oar appeared to be pointing to the place on the trunk where the Hidden Mickey was located.

Joey went to explore the living quarters and as he entered Mr. and Mrs. Robinson's bedroom, he found that carved into the headboard of the bed was a Hidden Mickey.

As he continued up the tree, he entered the dining area and found the plates and cups arranged to form a Mickey.

Remembering his fear of heights and predatory birds, Joey headed down the tree as quickly as possible and on to the next attraction.

The Enchanted Tiki Room

Nothing made Joey laugh harder than singing birds. So Joey entered the Enchanted Tiki Room and noticed that on the first bird perch, there was an upside down Mickey in the design.

There also appeared to be a Hidden Mickey on a forehead in the middle of a Tiki statue.

The show was a hit as Joey sang along with the birds.

The Magic Carpet of Aladdin

Remembering he needed to buy a gift for his mother, Joey went over to the gift shop across from Aladdin's Magic Carpet ride. Before entering, he found jewels in the ground and a few came together to form a classic Hidden Mickey.

It was about five in the evening and Joey looked at the list of Hidden Mickeys he had compiled. "I did it! That is all of them. I actually found all of the Hidden Mickeys in the Magic Kingdom." Joey knew this would be the perfect gift for his blind date tonight.

And it truly was. Joey's date went off without a hitch. They spent the night retracing the locations of all of the Hidden Mickeys thanks to the extra magic hours that kept the park open until 2am.

Chapter 8. The End of a Tale

This is where our story comes to an end. Joey found all of the Hidden Mickeys of the Magic Kingdom, discovered the girl of his dreams thanks to internet sensation Rodent Relations, and became known as the leading mouse expert of Hidden magic and secrets in the Magic Kingdom.

Even though this tale is over, the journey was just beginning. For, Joey realized that there are Hidden Mickeys all over the world that needed to be discovered. Some more in Florida, others in California, even more in Paris, Tokyo, and at Sea.

Join Joey on his other magical adventures as he travels the world to find Hidden Mickeys in some of greatest theme parks ever created.

Printed in Great Britain
by Amazon.co.uk, Ltd.,
Marston Gate.